PATSY CLINE: OUR FATHER'S OTHER DAUGHTER

PATSY CLINE: OUR FATHER'S OTHER DAUGHTER

✦

The never before told story of country music legend Patsy Cline's real father and her unknown family

Charlotte Brannon Bartles with Linda M. Sowers

iUniverse, Inc.
New York Lincoln Shanghai

PATSY CLINE: OUR FATHER'S OTHER DAUGHTER

The never before told story of country music legend Patsy Cline's real father and her unknown family

iUniverse books may be ordered through booksellers or by contacting:

iUniverse
2021 Pine Lake Road, Suite 100
Lincoln, NE 68512
www.iuniverse.com
1-800-Authors (1-800-288-4677)

Cover photos: Patsy Cline (left) and Charlotte Brannon Bartles (right) Patsy Cline photo/MICHAEL OCHS ARCHIVES.COM

ISBN-13: 978-0-595-37324-6 (pbk)
ISBN-13: 978-0-595-81722-1 (ebk)
ISBN-10: 0-595-37324-0 (pbk)
ISBN-10: 0-595-81722-X (ebk)

Printed in the United States of America

In memory of Richard Coe Bartles, Jay Richard Bartles, and Kristie Dawn
Brannon

Patsy, while you're singing in God's choir, I'll be waiting in the mist…

—Charlotte

Contents

PREFACE by Linda M. Sowers xi

CHAPTER 1   It's Time. 1

CHAPTER 2   Learning About Patsy 7

CHAPTER 3   Patsy's Roots and the Chester Brannon Family 21

CHAPTER 4   Visiting With Patsy 42

CHAPTER 5   Heartaches and Losses 54

CHAPTER 6   Sweet Dreams, Bittersweet Memories 63

PATSY'S ACHIEVEMENTS AND LEGACY 71

BIBLIOGRAPHY. 75

ACKNOWLEDGMENTS

Dick Hess • Jim Shaw • Jim Brannon (brother to our Dad)• Chuck and Lou Brannon • Allen and Larry Brannon (sons of Uncle Jim Brannon)• Donnie Dailey • Hazel Brannon Dailey • Dave Hess • Joe Hess • Ada Grimm and her sister Hilda • Reva Faircloth • Mick Caldwell • Anna Lou Brannon Marple • Nannie Brannon Unger • G. B. Cavender and his son Harold Cavender • Janet Henderson • Del Breakall • Ruella Brannon • Debbie Allanson Bruce • Frankie Allanson • Hugh and Ella Jean Brannon • Diane Brannon• Minnie Crouse • Mildred Crouse • Ed Fost • Jack Hill • Roy Weaver • Paul LaPaulte • Mary Klick Robinson • Mrs. Oscar Truax • Beverly McCormick Zimmerman • Gayle and Fay Brannon• Charlie Dick • Lorraine Myers • Cindy Hazen • Bruce Steinbicker • Ruth Anna Brannon Spencer • Leilani Zebart • Mary Lou Souders • Mr. And Mrs. Richard Carpenter • Mike and Mary Green • Donnie A. Sowers •

A special thank you to my brother Bob and my granddaughter Jayme for their assistance, unwavering encouragement, and support.

PREFACE

I was very puzzled when I read my first Patsy Cline biography. I couldn't understand why the Brannon name and the town of Hancock, Maryland were not mentioned. It did state that Sam Hensley was her father. That was news to me. I grew up knowing that Chester Brannon was her father. I lived in Hancock from 1956 until 1958, and I would hear the buzz whenever Patsy came to town to see him.

In 1958, my family moved from Hancock to a nearby location in Pennsylvania. The WCST radio station would fill our home with country music everyday, taking away the humdrum of doing chores. I would sing along with the hits of the day while ironing, and my sister would dance with the broom when a polka was played. My ears would perk up when I heard Patsy Cline's name on the radio or television. Our own local celebrity was making it big in the music business. I remember my disbelief and sadness when she died in 1963.

Long before the movie *Sweet Dreams*, I visited Patsy's grave in Winchester, VA. It troubled me to find it with only a few dried-up flowers lying near the marker. As soon as I returned home I ordered fresh flowers to be delivered to her grave.

During the early 80s, I was pursuing my own dream of becoming a singer, and Patsy was my inspiration as she's been and continues to be for countless others. I wrote a song about her influence on me and wanted her mother to hear it and be reminded that Patsy would never be forgotten. I contacted Charlotte Brannon Bartles, Chester Brannon's daughter, and asked her if she would get my recording of *Patsy* to Hilda Hensley.

PATSY
©1985 Words and Music by Linda M. Sowers

You touched me, Patsy, when I heard you on the radio and T.V.
You still have the pow'r that you had in sixty-three
When I heard the feeling in your voice
And I first felt its force

I knew I'd found the key
To free the song in me

You became a legend with style
A voice so strong it even reaches now
You were able to touch my heart with your melodies
You touched me, Patsy, you helped me see
That I can be just what I dream
When I say all I feel in a melody

You touch me Patsy, when I sing your songs, the music you made magic
Your special sound I'll always seek but never find
But I've got direction and my dreams
I won't fall behind
Inspired by you there's hope
In this life of mine

Charlotte did get my song to Hilda and told me in a letter that Hilda said she thought it was very "heartfelt." *Sweet Dreams* had been released by that time, and in that same letter she told me how upset Hilda was about the movie. We stayed in touch through letters and cards, but I didn't meet Charlotte until 1986 or 1987 when she came to the Capitol Theatre in Chambersburg, PA to see me perform on the Appalachian Jubilee, a traditional country music show. I immediately noticed her resemblance to Patsy. I had seen many pictures of Patsy and even thought they had the same smile. I never questioned her about her relationship to Patsy, and she never discussed it or brought it up. I concluded she wasn't comfortable talking about such a private matter and was glad I didn't force the subject.

In 1987, I received an invitation to attend the dedication ceremony of the Bell Tower, erected in honor of Patsy at the Shenandoah Memorial Park in Winchester where she is buried. I had no idea how I came to receive that invitation, but I seized the opportunity and went. It was overwhelming to be in the midst of such an event. Charlie Dick, Patsy's husband, and others spoke at the dedication in the afternoon. A banquet was held that evening at a nearby hotel. Musicians who had performed with Patsy were there. Vocalist Teresa Bowers sang a few of Patsy's signature songs. An article of clothing from *Sweet Dreams* was given away. Original records and other memorabilia were on display. Pictures of Patsy were sold; I bought two. I was one of a small group of people who remained after the banquet to watch videos of Patsy never seen by the public that Charlie had brought with him from Nashville. Charlotte Bartles did not attend these festivities. Since her relationship to Patsy was not known by the organizers of this event and not recognized by the ones who did know, she didn't receive an invitation.

My friends and I made a weekend of it, enjoying the town's Southern hospitality. And, despite the fact that only one year before the Winchester City Council voted against naming a street after Patsy, we found that the local citizens were very proud of their hometown music legend. A restaurant manager took the time to talk with us and even gave me one of Patsy's 8x10 publicity glossies. I heard my favorite tale of Patsy while I was shopping in a fabric store. The clerk explained how her grandfather had been an electric meter reader, and one day while reading the meter at Patsy's house, he observed her through a window practicing her singing in front of a mirror.

Charlotte and I maintained contact over the years, mostly through Christmas cards, and people and events in my life continued to have a Patsy connection. Odie Palmer, another big fan, was a member of the house band at the Appalachian Jubilee and would talk "Patsy" with me backstage. He was in the movie *Sweet Dreams*, cast as a member of the Kountry Krackers band, but had real life experience as part of a band backing Patsy. He told me of the time she said she wanted to "soar above the clouds." She was referring to her career, and Odie sadly pointed out the irony of that statement, in view of the fact she lost her life in a plane crash.

Winchester was the location for my 1990 wedding. My husband and I spent part of our honeymoon cruising around town, conducting our own tour of important Patsy landmarks such as Gaunt's Drugstore, Handley High School, and Kent Street. Except for the Bell Tower and Patsy Cline Memorial Highway (a short stretch of U.S. Route 522 South) there was little evidence that this had been Patsy's hometown. We stopped at the Visitors' Center to inquire about the location of a Patsy Cline exhibit only to be told there was none. Thankfully, that's changing now due to the past efforts of real estate developer Fern Adams, the Celebrating Patsy Cline, Inc. (a dedicated group of individuals determined to establish a permanent Patsy Cline museum), and the Always Patsy Cline Fan Club.

The years rolled by, and I still bought and listened to Patsy's music, excited when I came across one of her recordings I hadn't heard before. To my surprise, during a chance meeting with Charlotte in 2005, I found she was now talking openly about her kinship to Patsy. She expressed her desire to tell her story in a book, and I sensed urgency on her part to accomplish this. Soon the work began to bring this project to completion. It's been an unavoidable emotional roller-coaster for Charlotte. There were many tears, smiles, and "what if's." We visited the Stewart Bell Jr. Archives Room of the Handley Regional Library in Winchester, and upon entering, we noticed the large color portraits of Patsy hanging on the wall at the opposite end of the room. Charlotte immediately made a beeline to that wall, and the image of her standing there, wistfully looking up at Patsy, is an image that will forever remain stamped in my memory.

This book does not attempt to be a biography of Patsy Cline, several other books have done an excellent job of documenting the details of her life and career, but it is a significant revision to the biographies that have been written. There are new anecdotes that may give a little more insight into her personality and character. It is also the very personal story of the Brannon family, whose lives were intertwined with those of Patsy and her devoted mother, Hilda Patterson Hensley.

Patsy's all too brief life had an impact on so many lives, directly and indirectly. My singing career never materialized, but because Patsy's voice motivated me to sing, I do have treasured memories of exciting, fun times and of the wonderful people I met while learning how to "free the song in me." But nothing can compare to Charlotte Brannon Bartles' treasured, touching, and intimate memories of Patsy and her family that she is now sharing for the first time.

Linda M. Sowers

1

It's Time......

Patsy Cline, the legendary singer who died tragically on March 5, 1963, was my half-sister and the daughter of Hilda Hensley and my father Chester Brannon. It's a significant story that needs to be told. It's a part of my life experience and a part of my family's history. It's also a noteworthy part of Patsy's life that's been a missing chapter in all the biographies, one that could possibly help fans and friends know and understand her more. If Patsy were still with us, I do believe this truth would have already been revealed. She was a very forthright person and never made any attempts to hide the fact that she had a special relationship with my Dad. In Ellis Nassour's book, *Patsy Cline*, he stated "Two especially good friends of Patsy's—Dottie West and Del Wood—told me that Patsy Cline would want her life told 'like it was.'" Telling it "like it was" would include a long over-due public acknowledgment of her other family.

In 1996, Stuart E. Brown, Jr. and Lorraine F. Myers cowrote the book, *Singing Girl from the Shenandoah Valley*. Marie Brannon Allanson, my first cousin who was married to Hilda's half-brother Frank, was listed in the acknowledgments of Brown and Myers' book and she was also interviewed for Margaret Jones's book, *Patsy: The Life and Times of Patsy Cline*. I do not believe she ever mentioned my father to these biographers, which is understandable since this had been a delicate subject among some of my relatives for many years, and she was Hilda's sister-in-law. Hilda did not divulge the identity of Patsy's real father to any interviewers, and I believe one reason was her uncertainty about how my family would feel about this being brought out into the open. But, I'm sure the true reason was Hilda's reluctance to deal head on with this painful, very private part of her past in such a public way. It's a subject that her generation just didn't discuss outside the realm of trusted friends and loved ones.

In 1999, I received a letter from Mr. Brown telling me he would like more stories about Patsy and he added "or Hilda?!." He was a lawyer, genealogist, and researcher, and he had managed to track me down. For several reasons, mainly

1

family issues, I wasn't ready to talk openly about this and I ignored his request for information. I'm certain he knew about Chet Brannon and knew that Patsy called him Pop Brannon. Mr. Brown, who died in 2004, did complete another manuscript about Patsy. It has not been published but I have read it.

Since the 1950s, Patsy's connection to our family has been a well known "secret" in Hancock, MD and Winchester, VA, towns forty miles apart, and also in the surrounding tri-state area of Pennsylvania, Maryland, and West Virginia. More and more people are becoming aware of my family's connection to Patsy even though she's been gone all these years. Only a few who were directly involved with this story are still around. I'm now almost seventy-one years old; Mom, Dad, and Hilda Hensley have passed away, as have many who had been their friends and confidantes. So it's time to set the record straight. That hit home for me when I came across copies of notes someone had left in a library book about Patsy. These notes mentioned me by name as Patsy's half-sister and Chester Brannon as her father but they also contained a great deal of wrong information. There have been ridiculous and untrue stories floating around, such as the one about Patsy attending my father's funeral. I've even been told there was a rumor that she and I were twins. Sooner or later, this story would be told, but it needs to be told truthfully and as accurately as possible. If not, the crazy rumors and misinformation will make the truth appear to be nothing more than folklore. It's also important for me to have people understand that Dad and Patsy's relationship was more than a biological one. They knew each other and spent time together. Dad was very supportive and proud of Patsy.

CHESTER WARFIELD BRANNON, PATSY CLINE'S FATHER

His nicknames were "Chet" and "Ches." *Photo/Collection of Charlotte Brannon Bartles*

MAY • 5 7 •

HILDA PATTERSON HENSLEY, DEVOTED MOTHER OF PATSY CLINE

This picture was taken in 1957, an important year in her daughter's life. Patsy won first place on *Arthur Godfrey Talent Scout Show,* had a hit record with *Walking After Midnight,* and married Charlie Dick. *Photo/Collection of Bruce Steinbicker*

STUART E. BROWN, JR.
P.O. BOX 431
BERRYVILLE, VIRGINIA 22611

Mrs. Charlotte Brannon Bartles
227 Baptist Road
Hancock,
MD 21750

Would like any more stories about Betty! Or Hilda?!

STUART E. BROWN, JR.'S 1999 LETTER TO CHARLOTTE BARTLES

MARIE AND FRANK ALLANSON, JR.

Marie was the daughter of Tom and Lizzie Brannon. She was also Chet Brannon's niece and Patsy Cline's first cousin. Frank Allanson, Jr. was Hilda Hensley's half-brother. When Marie married Frank, she became Patsy's aunt. *Photo/ Courtesy of Debbie Allanson Bruce*

2

Learning About Patsy

Dad and I were visiting my Aunt Reva Faircloth, Mom's half-sister, when I learned I had a sister. Standing beside my Dad and holding his hand, I heard him tell Aunt Reva that Patsy was his daughter. He then turned, looked down at me and said, "And she's your sister." I was very young at the time, I don't remember exactly how old I was, but I was in either the second or third grade in school. At the time it really didn't sink in as to what it all meant. But I did understand I had a sister I didn't know and who didn't live with us. Anytime I would visit Aunt Reva and question her about this, she would say yes, that happened, and that's all she said.

While I was growing up, it was common to hear Mom and Dad talk about Patsy, what she was doing and where she'd be going, as anyone would talk about a member of the family. And I'm sure they discussed even more when I wasn't around. Mom was the one who talked to me most about Patsy and would at times refer to her as my sister. Dad would get it started when he'd make a comment that I looked or acted just like Patsy, then go off to work. Mom would pick it up from there.

Both my parents and Hilda, Patsy's mother, were from the Winchester area and belonged to the same circle of friends. Dad's romance with Hilda began at the home of his lifelong friend Raleigh Catlett, son of Phoebe Catlett, whose family employed Hilda. Mom told me that when Dad was still living at his parents' home, he came home drunk one night and fell into the hog pen. He must have been in pretty bad shape. Hilda jumped into the hog pen and stayed there all night to keep the hogs away from him. I have a hard time picturing that scene. Hilda was a very attractive woman, always well groomed, well dressed, and dignified. It had to have been nothing but pure love, devotion, and youth on her part to do something like that.

Hilda stayed for a time with my Uncle Tom, Dad's brother, and his wife Lizzie who lived across the field from Dad's home. Aunt Lizzie was pregnant with

Nannie and needed Hilda to baby-sit their children Marie, Chuck, and Anna Lou and to help out with other chores. Dad would jump the fence surrounding the property to get to Hilda. Nannie was born on January 29, 1932. Hilda was well into her pregnancy by the time she left my aunt and uncle's home. Mom told me Dad wanted to marry Hilda when he learned she was expecting, but Hilda refused. Patsy was born September 8, 1932. My mother discussed these things in a matter of fact way and never said anything nasty about Patsy and Hilda. I wish she had told me more. I should have asked more questions.

I've often thought maybe Hilda turned down Dad's marriage proposal because he was also dating my mother. In Hilda's eyes, that alone would cause serious doubts about his suitability as a husband. Perhaps she also had become all too familiar with his other less than desirable personality traits. And there's always the possibility that the circumstances were different or more complicated from what I was told or able to understand. I remember the time I overheard my parents discussing Patsy when they didn't know I was in the house. I heard Mom tell Dad, "You didn't claim her when she needed you, why are you claiming her now?" But I feel he always did claim her, at least from the time she was a little girl.

I can't even imagine how frightening it must have been for Hilda to find herself in such a situation, barely out of childhood herself, poor, pregnant and unmarried. She made a decision; I'm sure she felt it was the best one for her and her unborn child. Ellis Nassour, in his book *Honky Tonk Angel: The Intimate Story of Patsy Cline*, stated this about Hilda's marriage to Sam Hensley: "According to Hensley's diary, they married in 1929 after a whirlwind engagement." That diary entry was inaccurate, except for the "whirlwind" part. He was known for frequently moving from town to town, and it's my belief they couldn't have known each other for very long before saying "I do." They married at the Frederick County Courthouse in Winchester on September 2, 1932. Hilda was sixteen and Sam was forty-three. My Uncle Craven Coe Brannon was the court clerk and it was he who signed the marriage certificate. I wonder what thoughts were running through his mind. Did he know Hilda and was he aware his nephew was the father of the baby she was expecting? Virginia Patterson Hensley, who would later go by the name "Patsy," was born on September 8, 1932, six days after the wedding. Mom and Dad married in July 1934. I have no way of knowing for sure the details of what was going on with my parents and Hilda, but my first cousin Dave, son of Maud Hess, Dad's sister, filled me in on what he was told and he told me my mother wasn't herself around that time and there was "friction".

Aunt Maud was very loved by all her nieces and nephews. She was the one they turned to for comfort and care. Anytime I'd be upset and crying, she would wipe the tears from my eyes and say, "If you don't tell your old Aunt Maud what hurt you, how can I help you?" But she would never discuss Patsy with me. She and Hilda were very close friends, and because of that, I'm certain she knew the complete, inside story. She would be very kind when I asked questions but would only say she loved me and didn't want to hurt me. She told Dave the same thing, "I don't want to hurt Charlotte." I didn't understand it then, but there was more to it than just not wanting to hurt me.

The few things she did tell Dave made it more clear for me. She and Hilda were bosom buddies when they were young girls and would always walk together whenever they needed to go to Reynold's Store, a small village not far from Winchester. Dad and Hilda were smitten with one another, and Dad would throw stones at Aunt Maud to make her go away so he and Hilda could go off to be alone. Since Dad was also courting my mother at this time, Mom and Hilda ended up feuding. Aunt Maud got into the middle of it, and she and Dad had a major disagreement. After that, things were never the same between the two of them. There were years when Dad wouldn't speak to her, even though she lived only a mile from him. They didn't completely reconcile until they were senior citizens, and Dave believes it all stemmed from conflicts concerning Hilda. If I had repeated at home anything she said about Hilda and Patsy, it could have damaged her relationship with Dad even more. It could have also put a strain on her friendship with Hilda.

Larry Brannon, son of Dad's older brother Jim, told me about a letter Hilda had written to Dad. In it she wrote that her love for my father was "powerful enough to split a rail fence." It was found at my grandparents' home but disappeared. Allen, Larry's brother, said Uncle Jim told him that Dad was Patsy's father.

Marie, unlike my other cousins, never revealed to me what she knew. She was Hilda's sister-in-law as well as her good friend. Once I was at Marie's home and we went upstairs where I noticed a framed picture of Patsy on a table. I commented, "Oh, you have a picture of Patsy." Marie turned the picture over without saying anything, and that was that.

Of all his nieces, Dad was closest to Marie. She and Frank spent their honeymoon at our home. Dad couldn't resist teasing them and even tied bells to their bed. They would visit, go out for Sunday dinner together, and Marie and Frank would invite my parents to their home when she cooked country ham dinners, one of my father's favorite meals. They had a special bond, and maybe that bond was Hilda and Patsy. And because she was so close to both my father and Hilda, she probably didn't want to get involved in what had happened between them. That could explain why she avoided any mention of Patsy with me.

I don't recall meeting Patsy when we were little girls and teenagers. That could have been intentional on the part of our parents or maybe that's just the way it turned out due to life's circumstances. Regardless of the reason, it's still upsetting to me that she wasn't included in our lives when we were children. However, there may have been times when we were around each other on Sunday afternoons when family gathered at the home of my grandparents, E. Bruce and Priscilla Octavia Brannon, who lived on a large farm off Route 522 about 15 miles north of Winchester, VA. It was great place for us to visit. There were all kinds of animals there, including horses, and an apple orchard. Donnie Dailey, son of my father's sister Hazel, remembered that Hilda and Patsy visited my Grandma and Grandpa Brannon. Grandma would have Hilda sing to her, as Hilda had a beautiful singing voice. It was a large family, I was very young, and with so many kids running around, I wouldn't have realized who Patsy was if she had been there. Goodness, Uncle Tom had seven children and Aunt Maud had thirteen and that's not counting the children of my other aunts and uncles.

The first time I remember seeing and meeting Patsy was probably around 1955 when she came to my hometown, Hancock, MD, to sing at a carnival. We were both young married women at the time. Although she later divorced Gerald Cline, she kept the Cline name. She was very attractive, very jolly, and very nice to me, and I enjoyed her company. But it was obvious to me she wanted to hang out with Dad. After that, I would go see her perform anytime she was in the Hancock area. I would stand in front of the stage to watch her. I was so proud. She would walk the carnival grounds with Del Breakall, Janet Henderson, and me during her breaks. I didn't get the opportunity to know her better during those times as other people would always want to talk with her and get her autograph.

My cousin Dave, whose home was just over the hill from the Hancock carnival grounds, recalls the time he and a couple of his brothers sneaked off to the carnival. Shoeless, shirtless, but curious, he approached Patsy. She said, "You're one of Aunt Maud's boys" and rubbed his "burr" head. He was a little boy in total awe of her glittering cowgirl outfit and so entranced with her he didn't want to leave the carnival that night.

On one occasion, Patsy learned that a family had walked six miles to see her show. She was very touched by that and said the least she could do was drive them home. She asked me to go along. The family was so grateful they gave her a dog. It turned out to be a fairly quiet trip back to town, though. Patsy drove while I held the dog on my lap. In an attempt to get conversation started, I made an unflattering comment about Dale Turner's singing on the Town and Country Jamboree television show. Patsy didn't say anything, not a single word. Forty years later, I understood why she reacted that way. In the book, *Love Always, Patsy*, Patsy had written this about Dale in a letter:

"Her [Dale Turner] fan club is putting a big write-up in her book on me, and given your name to write to for joining the club, so I want you to do a little good for her too. She is a real sweet kid. She's not on records but she works every Sat night 3 hours T.V. with me on "Town and Country Time Jamboree." I'd love to help this kid in every way possible. I'll tell you about her sometime. She wants to be able to sing like me before she leaves this world. (Oh! she is well in health) but she knows and people all around her have made the mistake of telling her to "get a job at something she can do." I think this is awful. I've tried to help and encourage the girl, but she just sings out her nose too much. She says I've taught her a lot and so has at last got a set range now for working on T.V. For a long time she worked for nothing just so she could be part of the entertainment world." She was being a loyal friend to Dale, whom she cared about very much. That kind of loyalty, compassion, and desire to help others were a few of the reasons so many loved her.

Dad got to know her long before she started coming to Hancock and long before she was well known. He was a racecar driver, and when he raced in Winchester, he would occasionally take along my cousin Chuck Brannon, Uncle Tom's son, a popular tri-state area racecar driver in later years himself. Chuck told me that he had been with Dad a couple of times when Dad visited Hilda and Patsy. Dad would lift Patsy onto his lap and tell Chuck that she was "my daughter and your cousin." Chuck said the visits wouldn't last long but it was clear Dad's primary reason for being there was to see Patsy. I once expressed doubts to Chuck about Dad being Patsy's father. He answered, "There's no doubt about it, Charlotte, it's true," and, with a sly grin and twinkle in his eyes, he also said, "I don't tell everything I know."

Roy Weaver, one of Dad's friends, would haul Dad's racecar to the Winchester racetrack but make a stop so Dad could visit Hilda and Patsy. It was at a place located off Route 50. Roy said Dad walked a couple hundred yards to a white house on a hill, and Roy would wait in the truck while Dad visited.

Hilda and Patsy would also come to Hancock to see him. On one occasion, when Dad operated the Mobile service station, their car broke down and he arranged for Jack Hill to take them home while he repaired their car. He instructed Jack not to tell anyone.

He wasn't backward about telling his friends he was Patsy's father. One of those friends, Jim Shaw, told me how Dad would comment on how much Patsy and I looked alike. And Patsy added weight to the truthfulness of Dad's claim, when during a visit to Hancock, she spoke with Pearl Younker in Weaver's Restaurant. Pearl told me how she walked over to where Patsy was sitting and asked, "You're Patsy Cline, aren't you?" Pearl then added, "You're Chet Brannon's daughter." Patsy answered, "Yes, but I'm not allowed to talk about it." Those kind of comments spread like wildfire in a small town. As I grew up, people would ask me about Patsy and if Dad was Patsy Cline's father. It always bothered me when that happened. I didn't know that much about Patsy. Dad was the one who knew her and there were many things he didn't share with me. I wouldn't answer their questions, but would tell them to go ask my father.

As the years passed, more information came my way. At the sale of my Dad's property following his death in 1984, two women I had never seen before in my life called me out of the crowd. I thought maybe there was something wrong about the sale, but I soon found out they had only come to the sale to talk with me concerning a more personal subject. The women were sisters, Ada Grimm and Hilda Catlett, members of Mom, Dad, and Hilda's old crowd of friends from Winchester. Mrs. Catlett was still a friend to Hilda and proceeded to tell me that Hilda had told her that my father, Chet Brannon, was also Patsy's father. She advised me to tell Hilda that she told me this and then Hilda would tell me the rest of the story. The sisters also said that many of the older people who lived around Reynold's Store knew the story and referred to Patsy as Patsy Brannon.

Geraldine "Mina" McCormick's son and my son Jay attended Hancock High School together. One day I called Geraldine about a school matter. The conversation took a different turn when she told me she had a picture of Dottie West she wanted to give me. She had a special reason for wanting me to have this picture. I can't remember how, when, or where she met Dottie, but while she was getting Dottie's autograph, Dottie asked Geraldine where she was from. When Geraldine told her Hancock, MD, Dottie said, "Patsy Cline told me she had a sister in Hancock, MD."

TOM AND LIZZIE BRANNON'S CHILDREN

Front row, left to right: Hugh "Punch," Benny, Nannie. Second row, left to right: Charles "Chuck," Belva "Marie," and Anna Lou. They are standing on the porch of their home. Hilda stayed at their home when Lizzie Brannon was pregnant with Nannie, 1931–1932.
Photo/Courtesy of Hugh and Ella Jean Brannon and daughter Diane

TOM AND LIZZIE BRANNON'S FORMER HOME AS IT LOOKS TODAY

Photo by Charlotte Bartles

GRANDMA AND GRANDPA BRANNON'S HOME

Left to right: Marie, Chuck, and Anna Lou. Aunt Maud Hess is sitting on the porch. It doesn't show in this picture, but the home was a large, two story, wooden house. There was a barn on the property, hogpens, and an outhouse that tilted.

Photo/Courtesy of Hugh and Ella Jean Brannon and daughter Diane

A VERY YOUNG AUNT MAUD

Maud was Chester "Chet" Brannon's sister. On the day she was born, her family's work horse "Maud" dropped dead and she inherited the name. She and Hilda Patterson Hensley were childhood friends and remained close friends throughout their lives. *Photo/Courtesy of Joe Hess*

DAVE HESS, SON OF MAUD HESS

Dave shared with Charlotte Brannon Bartles stories his mother had told him about her brother Chet Brannon's romantic triangle with Gladys Scroggins and Hilda Patterson. *Photo/Courtesy of Dave Hess*

CRAVEN COE BRANNON

Craven Coe was Chet Brannon's uncle. He signed Hilda Patterson and Samuel Hensley's marriage certificate. *Photo/Stewart Bell Jr. Archives Room, Handley Regional Library, Winchester, VA/Collection of Charlotte Brannon Bartles*

HILDA AND SAM'S MARRIAGE CERTIFICATE SIGNED BY CRAVEN COE
BRANNON, CHET BRANNON'S UNCLE.

Private Collection of Charlotte Brannon Bartles

CHARLES "CHUCK" BRANNON

Chuck, nephew of Chet Brannon, was also a racecar driver and still enjoys the sport.

Photo/Courtesy of Charles Brannon

3

Patsy's Roots and the Chester Brannon Family

According to written family records, Chester Brannon's great, great grandfather, John Brannon came from Ireland. His wife Rebecca was from England. They married in Pennsylvania, settled down in Frederick County, Virginia, and raised twelve children. Most of the children went West. The three children who remained in Frederick County were Levi, Robert, and Rachael. Family records describe Robert as the "famous old tavern keeper of Winchester" and "for fifty years he had been before the public and owned large interests in every enterprise." Those enterprises included the tavern, a livery business, farming, and one of their sons, Evan R., was a supervisor of Frederick County. Levi married Ruth Gray, had twelve children and lived on the Brannon farm in the Pughtown section. A son, Levi Gray, had three sons. J. William was in the mercantile business and owned part of the home tract. Craven Coe Brannon was Commissioner of Revenue for Northern District of Frederick County. He was Frederick County Court clerk from 1920 until 1939, and his picture hangs on a wall in the Frederick County Courthouse to this day. E. Bruce was described as a prosperous farmer. The family records concluded, "All are worthy men and maintaining the good name of their father." E. Bruce Brannon was Dad's father and my grandfather.

Edward Bruce Brannon married Priscilla Octavia Zeilor, whom everyone called "Oc." Their children were James, Thomas Jefferson, Matthias Gray, Harry Kenneth, Zeilor Lynn, Mildred Lee, Hazel Marie, Maud Virginia, and Edward Bruce, and my father, Chester "Chet" Warfield Brannon. Uncle James was the oldest. Uncle Ed died from cancer before he was thirty. All are now deceased.

Grandma Brannon, whose mother was a full-blooded Shawnee Indian, had a very dark complexion and very dark eyes. She couldn't stand her clothes touching her and always wore baggy ones. Her hairdo was most unusual. She would take a portion of her hair and knotted it to make a ponytail high on the top of her head.

She never would allow her picture to be taken, but someone managed to get a picture of her feeding the hogs, her unusual ponytail very visible. She went to her grave not knowing her family had this picture. She smoked a corncob pipe but didn't want anyone outside the family to see her smoke. If someone stopped by unexpectedly, she'd head for the nearest closet so she could hide the evidence. Naturally, I had to try out her pipe at least once. I got sick, so once was enough.

She was fun loving, spunky, an excellent cook, a hard worker, and unforgettable. There was always food on her table with a cloth thrown over it. I never once saw the table without food. She was a softie when it came to her grandchildren and often took up for them even when they were in the wrong. Once, Uncle Tom's kids were to do some work at the farm and tried to pull a fast one to get out of it. They arrived with their toes "bandaged," saying their feet were too sore for them to do the work. It was Uncle Ed who had to expose their little scheme to Grandma. When Uncle Craven Coe died, I wanted to go the funeral with my parents but was forced to stay with Grandma and Aunt Maud. I threw a fit. In an effort to shut me up, Grandma gave me a penny. Then I saw the funeral procession pass by. That triggered another tantrum. And I didn't give a hoot about the penny anymore; I pitched it out into the yard. All I wanted was to be with Mom and Dad. Grandma must have understood how miserable I felt because she didn't punish me for my bad behavior. I never did find that penny.

I inherited Grandma's dark hair and dark eyes, as did Patsy, Uncle Tom, and Marie. My father had a fairer complexion than Marie and Uncle Tom but he still had the dark eyes.

Grandpa Brannon's personality was more easygoing and quiet than Grandma's. I think he was always smiling. My fondest memories are the times just the two of us rode the horses down to the creek for watering. One day my cousin and I "went missing" when we decided we'd go down by the creek to play. Everyone was looking for us. Grandpa was the one who found us, but he just stood quietly and patiently at the top of the hill watching over us until we were through playing.

I've been told he was quite the singer, and Uncle Ed played the guitar and sang. My father definitely didn't inherit their musical abilities. In the book, *Honky Tonk Angel: The Intimate Story of Patsy Cline,* in response to a question about how Patsy got interested in country music, Hilda is quoted as saying "It must have been in her blood" and "She didn't take after me or her daddy." I agree with her about Patsy's daddy. I heard him when he tried to sing, and he couldn't carry a tune in a bucket. But from all reports, Hilda was a gifted singer, and there existed some musical ability on the Brannon side. And I believe the Brannon genes contributed to Patsy's strong work ethic, perseverance, and drive to succeed.

My grandparents' home was torn down when more of Route 522 was built. They were gone by that time, both had died in 1943, within three months of one another. It was painful for their children to watch the home place vanish. No more memories would be made there, a place that had been a haven for the Brannon family. Tears were shed.

Dad was born in July 1912, but there was confusion about the exact day. He was born at home and two different dates were recorded. He always joked about having two birthdays. We celebrated his birthday on the 19th, but his Social Security records give his birth date as July 21st. Mom was beautiful, petite Gladys Scroggins from Winchester, born July 6, 1916. I know little about their courtship, only that they ran with the same crowd of friends and that Dad had been very involved with Hilda while he was dating my mother. I heard from Aunt Mildred Crouse, one of Dad's sisters, that he was a ladies' man from the beginning. I imagine being a racecar driver made him seem glamorous and exciting to the young ladies. He had a daredevil personality and good looks. He continued racing in Winchester and at other local racetracks for many years after his 1934 marriage to Mom.

After they wed, my parents lived with Uncle Jim and Aunt Jessie Brannon in Winchester. I was born there on September 21, 1934. Dr. Lewis M. Allen, the same doctor who delivered Patsy, delivered me (Incidentally, I've heard that he also delivered the baby who would become the controversial Duchess of Windsor, Wallis Simpson). It's possible that Aunt Jessie and Hilda were related; Aunt Jessie's maiden name was Patterson and her daughter Ruth Anna told me Aunt Jessie visited Hilda.

My parents and I moved from Winchester to Hancock, MD when I was eleven months old so Dad could take a job as a mechanic at a garage there. Dad rented a house across the road from the Park 'n Dine Restaurant for three months, then moved us to a house across from the Methodist Church, the same one that still stands there today. Eventually, he went into business with Orie Davidson doing mechanic work in a garage located behind where the Lockhouse Restaurant is now. Dad only had a fourth grade education but that never held him back. He had great mechanic skills and was also great at math.

But it wasn't all work and no adventure with Dad and Orie. At the racetrack in Winchester, a stunt was performed requiring someone to sit on the hood of a car while the driver drove through a big, burning fence. Orie was to be on the hood but chickened out. So Dad rode on the hood and Orie drove. Dad got through the fence just fine, but flames flew back on Orie.

Another stunt was for two cars to hit head on, while each was going at a speed of fifty miles an hour. They would put a mattress in the backseat and jump over onto the mattress just in the nick of time before the cars crashed. Dad said he came out of the wreckage many times spitting blood. Fortunately, neither one was ever seriously injured.

Dad took a job in Mount Holly, NJ when my brother Bob, born in 1940, and I were very young. He once took all of us along with him for a visit. We stayed for a week or two, but I was so young all I remember about that visit is the cuckoo clock in the home where we stayed. Every hour, on the hour, I was standing in front of that clock waiting for the bird to make his appearance. Dad was gone for about a year during the 1940s when he and a few other men from Hancock went to Puerto Rico for work. This was after he had tried unsuccessfully to enlist in the various branches of the service. He was rejected because of his flat feet.

It was sometime in the late 40s or early 50s that Dad began renting and operating a Mobile service station at the east end of town, near Hepburn's packing house. The man he hired to help lived in an apartment above the station. He put me to work for him pumping gas, and he taught me how to change oil. While my friends were out having fun, I was learning all about carburetors! Around 1952, he bought the land across the road and built a radiator shop, a glass shop, a Mobile service station, an icehouse, a combination grocery store and fruitstand, and our home. He built a successful business, even though his mouth could get ahead of him. His language was downright embarrassing when he lost his temper, which could happen in a heartbeat, but his customers kept coming back because he was so good at anything he did. He worked very long hours and so did I.

Dad joined the Lion's Club, served as a town councilman for twelve years, and was the county deputy sheriff for a brief time in the early 50s.

Hancock was a bustling little town then. You were lucky if you could find a parking place on Friday and Saturday nights when people from the surrounding areas would come into town to do their banking, stock up on groceries, and shop for household goods and clothing at such stores as G. C. Murphy's and Silco's. The sidewalks were crowded as the shoppers strolled from one store to the next. It was also a time to see and be seen by neighbors and friends and to do some socializing.

Dad's business was a busy, demanding place, and I worked there seven days a week. I would get up early on Saturday mornings so I could get the housework done and get groceries before I started working at the store and fruit stand. Mom had poor health due to the breathing problem she'd had since childhood and usually only helped with the fruit stand. I would pick peaches for the fruit stand by moonlight. We also traveled to Baltimore to get fruit. Dad hired people at the docks to load the truck but when we got home I was expected to unload it. One night I started unloading, but I was too exhausted. The next morning Dad found me asleep among the watermelons. He didn't have the heart to scold me for that one. Bob also worked long and hard at the businesses when he was old enough. It wasn't a choice on our part, we had to do it, and we didn't get paid. But Dad made sure we had a nice home, nice clothes, cars, and an education. Around 1958, the state took the house and businesses when Interstate 70 came through, and I grinned from ear to ear. Dad set about building a new home and garage on Pennsylvania Ave. in the town limits of Hancock. Folks said they never saw a house go up so fast.

Dad could be tough on me, but he was my best teacher when I was a young girl, and I was always learning something. I'll never forget the time I was showing a friend how to drive. She hit another car head on. As soon as we were released from the hospital, while I was still in bloody clothes and had glass in my hair, Dad made me get into the car and drive it to the other end of town and back. I was terrified and shaking, but I did it. I was so upset with him. When I returned from my little drive, I asked him why on earth he forced me to do that. He told me that if I hadn't, I never would have had the nerve to drive again. I do believe he was right.

He always made sure I had a car, although I was never sure how long I would get to keep it. He traded my '36 Chevrolet to George "Mick" Caldwell for a gun. One day I drove some of my friends to Martinsburg, WV in an old Ford and the brakes kept giving out. We'd stop, pour in more brake fluid, and managed to make it home. Dad took that car into the field, set it on fire, and declared, "You won't get killed in that car."

Dad didn't openly display affection. I don't remember him hugging or kissing me. And if he were in the wrong about something, he would never apologize. Instead he would hand me some cash. Of course, that's not what I really wanted, but I guess it was his way of saying he was sorry. That's how he would handle apologies to Mom, too.

Dad wasn't home much and rarely offered any explanation. One night he did tell us he was late getting home because the car he was racing had gone over a bank. He would go to Winchester often and there were nights he didn't come home. I believe he always had a girlfriend or two and that accounted for some of his time away from home.

On one occasion, he was seen sitting with one of his lady friends, drunk, on the front porch of her house on Main Street. A man, I won't mention his name, who witnessed this came up to me and asked in a mocking voice, "Where's your Daddy?" and made other rude remarks as if it were my fault. That same lady friend gave Dad a leather jacket one year for Christmas. Mom threw it into the stove while informing him that was one coat he'd never wear. I saw the flames shoot out from the stove when the coat hit the fire.

But Mom didn't give up. She was always there for my brother Bob and me. When I was older, I once asked her why she didn't leave him. Her answer was "Where would I go?" At least with Dad, she had her family and financial security. She never had an easy life. When she was a little girl, a bout with the whooping cough damaged her lungs causing a lifelong condition known as bronchiectasis. I'm sure the money hadn't been there for her to receive proper medical care. She lost her mother during the flu epidemic of 1918. That was something else she and Hilda had in common. Hilda's father died during that same epidemic. Mom's father remarried but more misfortune came his way when he had a stroke that left him paralyzed and the family impoverished. She ended up being jostled from pillar to post. Most of the time she was with an aunt and uncle who viewed her as their personal servant. As Bob says, she was their "Cinderella." I guess when she met Dad, he seemed like a prince on a white horse coming to her rescue.

In spite of everything Mom experienced, I never heard her say a bad word about anyone; she set a good example and trained us well. She took us to the Methodist Church on Sundays, even though Dad wouldn't go with us. He declared he knew the Bible. I never needed any encouragement to attend. I always felt the Lord was with me and I wanted to be in church.

Church and school activities, along with running around with my friends in my car, made up most of my social life when I was a teenager. Saturday nights were always special back then. I'd dress in my better clothes, get all dolled up, and then go out for the evening with my friends. We usually ended up at the movies. I enjoyed country music, which was very popular in our area, and listened to it on the radio. I didn't buy that many records. Later on I listened to other types of music, fell in love with Elvis, and bought Patsy's records. My favorite one of hers was *If I Could See the World Through the Eyes of a Child*. Dad would have me sing along with the radio when we went for Sunday drives. It made me wonder if he wanted me to be a singer like Patsy. I always felt he wanted me to be like her. I sang solos at church and was a member of the church choir and the high school Glee Club, but I never had a desire to sing professionally.

Dad never hovered over me, dictating how I should dress or asking where I'd been. I'm not even sure he knew who I was dating. He knew he could trust and rely upon Mom to make sure things were the way they were supposed to be. But he'd still hand out tough punishment that often didn't fit the crime if we did something that made him mad.

When I was around thirteen, I was confined to my bedroom for three weeks, except for meals and to use the bathroom, because I balked at getting Mom a jar of tomatoes from the basement. The basement was dark, full of water and I was afraid it was also full of snakes. Bob refers to the time he was riding in the car with Mom and Dad on their way to the racetrack on a Saturday night. He was eating an ice cream cone. The window was down, and the wind blew some melting ice cream onto Mom's new dress. Dad was furious. He stopped the car, pulled Bob out, threw him over a bank, got on top of him, and drew back his fist to strike him. Mom screamed at him and he backed off. Throughout that night at the race, Bob said Dad couldn't buy him enough hotdogs, sodas, snow cones, and other goodies. That was his usual way of making up for something he had done wrong.

He was especially harsh with Bob, more so than with me. I don't know why. Maybe it was due to my being older than Bob, and because of that, I had been able to help him more during the early years of the businesses. But Mom did her best to make up for the affection and attention Bob didn't get from Dad. Today, Bob refers to him as "Ches," not Dad

I think he tried to make Bob into a daredevil like himself. Dad got a pilot's license to fly small planes. He would have Bob drive the truck when they went to the airstrip near Hancock. Bob was only around ten or eleven years old then, and his feet barely touched the pedals. Dad would take him up in the plane and occasionally scare the daylights out of him. One time he purposely sent the plane into a nosedive, took his hands off the controls and said, "You'd better get that stick, boy." Bob did as he was told, and there were times when he would be the one flying the plane along the Potomac River.

Dad had a terrible temper and didn't hold it back. I can't remember what set him off, but I do remember he once threw a dish of fried potatoes across the room, and that's just one example of how he'd act when his temper controlled him. And when that rage was fueled by liquor, it was even worse. There were times when we were afraid of him.

I didn't like school, I found the teachers' lectures too boring, and so I quit school when I was in the 11th grade. I was able to get my G.E.D. in three months and later on graduated from Hagerstown Business College. One thing Dad requested before he died was to see my G.E.D. So now I think maybe he was disappointed when I quit high school.

Bob not only graduated from high school, but also went on to graduate from Frostburg State Teachers' College. He taught for a time in Beltsville, MD, but decided he wasn't cut out for teaching. He returned to Hancock and began a career in finance, which would require him to relocate several times.

I continued to work for Dad. I once had a job at a medical book publishing company, but he told me he would pay as much as I was being paid there if I would come back to work for him. And that's what I did. I did his bookkeeping even after his businesses closed at the east end of town and he only had the radiator and glass shop business.

I met my husband, Dick Bartles, through a group of friends I ran around with from Clear Spring, MD. We got married in 1953, right before he went into the army. It was a no fuss wedding. The preacher who lived across the street from Dick's mother in Clear Spring married us in his home.

I joined Dick in Louisiana when he was stationed there. It was a lean time. Mom and Dad would send boxes of groceries, and, as a joke, Dad would put in things like sardines and lollipops. But the joke was on him. We loved the sardines. They tasted as good as steak to us, and then we could have lollipops for dessert. After two months, I was back at my parents' home and lived with them until Dick was out of the service.

I didn't have any way of knowing it then, but those years before Mom died would be the best years I had with my father. His last years brought much heartache.

Dad did have a big heart and concern for others and I'm sure he felt remorse for some of his actions. He just had a hard time expressing those kinds of emotions in words and took the easy way out by substituting money for the words "I'm sorry" or "I love you." He provided very well for Mom and us kids. If he knew a relative or friend needed money, he would take care of that himself. When he'd be concerned about someone, he would send me to find out what they needed. And he could be the jokester and lots of fun to be around, but he was either all glad or all mad. There was no middle ground with his moods.

There were times we could count on him being "all glad." That would be when Patsy came to visit.

GRANDMA PRISCILLA OCTAVIA ZEILOR BRANNON

She was the wife of E. Bruce Brannon and Chester Brannon's mother. She and her husband raised ten children. *Photo/Collection of Charlotte Brannon Bartles*

GRANDPA E. BRUCE BRANNON WITH GRANDCHILDREN

Children sitting, left to right: Allen Brannon, Randolph Dailey, Mick Dailey, Donnie Dailey. Standing, left to right: Ruth Anna Brannon Spencer, standing directly behind Ruth Anna is Vivian Crouse Hinckle, Grandfather Brannon holding Priscilla Dailey, Marie Brannon, Anna Lou Brannon. Donnie Dailey remembered Patsy and Hilda visiting his grandparents. Grandma and Granddad Brannon died within three months of each other in 1943. *Photo/Courtesy of Joe Hess*

CHET BRANNON

Photo/Collection of Charlotte Brannon Bartles

GLADYS SCROGGINS BRANNON

She wed Chet Brannon in 1934. The license plate on the car shows that this photo was taken in 1932 when she was 16 years old. *Photo/Collection of Charlotte Brannon Bartles*

CHET AND GLADYS BRANNON

The young couple appear very serious in this photo taken during their early years in Hancock, MD. *Photo/Collection of Charlotte Brannon Bartles*

BABY CHARLOTTE BRANNON

Daughter of Chet and Gladys Brannon and half-sister of Patsy Cline. This photo was taken in Winchester before she and her parents moved from Winchester, VA to Hancock, MD.

Photo/Collection of Charlotte Brannon Bartles

CHARLOTTE BRANNON BARTLES

She was 14 years old and recovering from the strep throat when this photo was taken.
Photo/Collection of Charlotte Brannon Bartles

CHARLOTTE BRANNON BARTLES, STYLISH TEENAGER

Photo/Collection of Charlotte Brannon Bartles

RACING DAREDEVIL CHET BRANNON

He never lost his love for fast cars and racing. *Photo/Collection of Charlotte Brannon Bartles*

CHARLOTTE AND DICK BARTLES, YOUNG MARRIED COUPLE

Photo/Collection of Charlotte Brannon Bartles

TWENTY-SOMETHING CHARLOTTE

Photo/Collection Charlotte Brannon Bartles

ROBERT W. BRANNON
"BOB"

Son of Chet and Gladys Brannon and Patsy Cline's half-brother. While he was in college, his father gifted him with a 1962 Chevy with a 409 engine. *Photo/Collection of Charlotte Bartles*

CHET BRANNON'S BUSINESS IN HANCOCK, MD

Portion of building to the far left was the radiator shop, top portion of building with the two windows was where Chet cut glass, adjoining the radiator shop was the service station, adjoining the service station on the right was the ice house. The next building to the right was the fruit stand, store, and above the store was an apartment. The Brannon home is not seen in this picture. It was located a short walking distance from the fruit stand and store. *Photo/Collection of Charlotte Brannon Bartles*

4

Visiting With Patsy

The following are my brother Bob's recollections of Patsy:

"It was a bright, sunny, Saturday afternoon. I played basketball on our high school team. A Saturday practice session was rare. But all the team enjoyed the game, so we didn't complain.

When I got home I noticed a strange vehicle in the driveway. As I entered the house Mom was washing dishes in the sink. I spoke to her and told her I was going back to put my gym bag in my bedroom. Mom said to be quiet, adding, "Patsy's lying on your bed taking a nap.

As I quietly, almost on my tiptoes, walked back to my bedroom the door was partially closed. I remember Patsy was lying diagonally across the bed sleeping in her dress and her red high heel shoes lay on the floor as if she had kicked them off and let them lay where they fell.

About a half hour after leaving my gym bag in my bedroom, Patsy got up and walked out into the kitchen. Mom and I were sitting at the kitchen table, and Chet, a nickname everyone called my father, stepped into the kitchen, having come over from his business next door. Patsy smiled broadly and made idle chat about getting a good rest. She was telling jokes about her times traveling on the road. She stood with her back to the kitchen sink and the heels of her hands resting on the edge of the counter surrounding the sink.

I noticed she had a hard time talking without cussing. She would look in Mom and my direction when she would let one slip with a look of apology. She could also get deep into conversation using body language to emphasize a point. What I remember most was as she finished a small joke, she stomped her foot, wearing the red high heels, hard on the floor, laughing out loud. The heel of one of the shoes broke off. She looked abruptly down at what happened and with a shrug of her shoulders said, "Oh hell, they only cost $80. I'll just get another pair (At the time women were paying about $20-$25 for a pair of high heel shoes)

My father enjoyed playing poker in the basement with friends. I used to play a lot with them. One evening about six of us had gathered in the basement playing what came to be an every weekend poker game. I heard the door open and Mom yelled down, "Chet, Patsy's here, can you come up?" Before he could get up out of his chair, Patsy appeared in the doorway. At this time she had become a well-known country western singer. All stared in disbelief as she smiled and said "Hello." I still have a friend who writes me and tells me about that evening Patsy Cline stood right in front of him. Although he never cared much for country western music, it created a desire to listen to her songs. Her singing had an inspiring quality that won him over.

Another day Patsy had stopped by and came into the house looking for my father. She said she was with Jimmy Dean and others and were on their way down to sing on stage at the Washington Jamboree. She was just getting her career started, and I later found out my father was helping her financially from time to time.

My father was a member of the Hancock Lions Club, and would ask Patsy to come to carnivals and supply the entertainment for a night. She would come without question and sing. I'm not sure if she ever took any money for her performances.

I was going to teachers' college and took art as my major. As a project in one of my classes I drew a horse's head and colored it using a sponge technique and water colors. Patsy and her husband Charlie Dick had stopped by for a visit on the weekend. I brought the drawing home and had it lying on the dining room table. Patsy admired my work and said she was re-doing a room in her house in a western theme. She asked me if she could have it. Myself, just getting started in the field of art, was appreciative that anyone could like what I had drawn. With no hesitation I gladly handed it to her. She said, "when I get it framed I'll hang it in the room." I have no idea where the drawing is today.

I came to know Patsy by the many visits to our home. Other than she was a singer who came from Winchester, VA, my parents' hometown, I didn't know a great deal about her. My older sister Charlotte was more knowledgeable and more fully aware of Patsy I found out later.

Years after the tragic death of Patsy with the advice of relatives and acquaintances, we are telling our story as only we know it."

——Robert "Bob" Brannon

I can add a few more details to Bob's recollections, but that was going on fifty years ago and too many of the little particulars have faded from my memory. I never kept a diary to record events and circumstances; our family seldom took pictures.

Another performance Dad arranged for Patsy was at a parachute jump at the airstrip near our home, in Hancock, WV. One parachute didn't open and a man was injured. She also sang at the Hancock Drive-In Theater.

I never had a problem with Dad giving money to Patsy. As her father, it was his responsibility to do that. I'm confident he had done that all along, and I have reason to believe he helped Hilda as well. Bob didn't even know that Patsy was our half-sister until he was almost through college. I was the one who spilled the beans. Mom and Dad never told him. He only thought she came to our house because she was associated with our parents' friends in Winchester.

I wish I could remember more about her visits, especially the conversations. The shoe heel that broke was made of a crystal looking plastic and filled with little beads. When it broke, beads rolled everywhere. For weeks after that, we'd find a few of those beads each time we swept the floor. I believe it was during this same visit she cut her finger while opening a Coke bottle. She was enroute to do a television show with Arthur Godfrey, who Dad referred to as "Awful Godfrey," and told us to pay close attention while she sang on the show, as she would hold her finger up that had the Band-Aid. And she did, just for us.

We didn't always have the chance to see her when she stopped by as I was married and no longer living at home, and Bob was busy with school. She liked to rest on Bob's bed before heading off to sing. But Mom or Dad would usually mention to us that she'd been there. It was obvious that she came only to see Dad. Bob said one day she stepped into the house, saw that Dad wasn't there, asked Bob where she could find him, and then left without making any further conversation. She would often stop at his business and not come to the house.

The word would spread when Patsy was in town, and soon cars would start lining up across the road from our house with people hoping to get a glimpse of her. Occasionally, my father would go over and invite them in to meet her. I don't think anyone ever took him up on his offer, except for George "Mick" Caldwell, who rented my Dad's service station. It turned out to be quite a memorable experience for him. Wearing nothing but a red bra and a red half-slip, Patsy nonchalantly emerged from another room to greet him. She was in the middle of getting dressed for a show. Years later, with a very nice smile on his face, he told me "it didn't look too bad, either." They talked for five or ten minutes about her career. He didn't get her autograph and says, "I never dreamed it would be the last time I'd ever see her." Dad answered "yes" when Mick asked him if he was Patsy's father.

Dad always made sure his good friend and fellow town councilman Leo "Jim" McCormick knew when Patsy was in town. Jim owned McCormick's Tavern in

Hancock and his favorite song, *Walking After Midnight*, was on his jukebox. He would usually take his young daughter Beverly with him to meet Patsy in the parking lot at Dad's business. Dad, Jim, and Patsy did the talking, while Beverly checked out Patsy's pretty, fancy dresses, the skirt held out by crinolines. But she did some listening, too, and I learned from her that our dads had partied with Patsy and Hilda a time or two in Winchester. She said she was around fifteen when her father told her their friend Chet was Patsy's father.

Almost every Saturday night between 1955–1957, my parents would make the hundred-mile trip to Washington, DC to see her perform on the Town and Country Jamboree television show. Up until that time, they rarely went out together on Saturday nights. It was a live show, and many people from the tri-state area would attend so they could be seen on TV. Many held up signs with the names of the towns they were from. I went with them once, and my most vivid memory is Jimmy Dean announcing, "Hey, you people from Hancock, your sign's upside down." Sure enough, we had it upside down. Most Saturday nights I was at home watching her on television

Dave told me that there was some jealousy on Mom's part concerning Patsy during this period of time. If there was, she hid it well and I certainly never sensed jealousy when Patsy was around. Did Patsy feel there was jealousy and tell her mother who in turn could have conveyed that to Aunt Maud? It's one of those things we'll never know. But it would have been only human of Mom if she had felt a little jealousy. After all, Patsy's mother was a woman for who Dad had deep feelings and he adored Patsy. He kept her 8x10 glossy picture, autographed to "Pop and Mom Brannon" in their bedroom, and kept it there until the day he died.

It was apparent Dad and Patsy were becoming very attached to one another during the mid to late 1950s. In 1957, my parents were invited to Patsy's wedding to Charlie Dick. They didn't attend the wedding, but did go to the reception at the Mountainside Inn.

No doubt about it, when Patsy was around, you knew she was special, a star. Anytime I saw her at the house she was dressed up, wearing high heels, and bright red lipstick. Dad would be lit up like a Christmas tree, charming, funny, and on his best behavior.

I was at my parents' home the day Patsy visited them with her husband Charlie, their daughter Julie, Hilda, and Hilda's other daughter, Sylvia. Julie was just a toddler. Hilda looked very attractive, slender, but had curves like Patsy. I fried chicken for our dinner, while my father and Patsy held the floor with their conversation, jokes, and laughter. Patsy told one ornery joke, using her finger to represent a male body part. Hilda looked a little embarrassed. At one point, Patsy sat with me on the sofa. We talked about Brenda Lee, and Patsy told me she was a very good friend of hers and that Brenda was older than she looked. That visit was the last time I'd be with Patsy. I don't know for sure if she ever returned to Hancock after that visit. Dad never told me if she called or wrote to him.

After they left that night, Mom told me she could really see how much Patsy and I looked alike when we sat side by side on the sofa. Remarkably, we had both inherited Dad's features even though we had different mothers. I can really see the resemblance when I compare the few, early pictures of myself with her early publicity photos. We had the same face shape, nose, mouth, dark hair and dark eyes. Her lower lip, like mine, was fuller than the upper lip. She applied her lipstick above the upper lip line, which was a common makeup trick in those days, and it gave the appearance of very full lips. I've noticed in her later pictures she didn't use that technique as much.

I would watch her on television and feel so lonely for her, knowing she was my sister, but not really knowing her. I sincerely believe she would have liked to know me better, too. She always sought me out whenever I would be at one her shows. We just didn't have that many opportunities to talk privately or spend any amount of time together. I regret that I didn't somehow find a way to be with her more. But, she had things to do and places to go. It's astounding when I think about all she did. We were both young, and I never dreamed there wouldn't be time for us in the future.

When she was at the house, she was very nice to Bob and me but didn't have much to say to us. It was probably because Dad controlled all the conversation while she was there. I wasn't bold enough to initiate any conversation when Dad was in the room. I was afraid there would be consequences if I said something he didn't like. Even after his death, it took quite a few years to overcome my fear of speaking up. I now think I'm more like Patsy in that department.

One weekend, my husband Dick, his brother Donnie, and I decided to go to one of her shows at the Baltimore Civic Area. She sat at our table with us when she wasn't on stage. That was another instance of being with her and not getting to know her any better. She, Dick, and Donnie were drinking, talking, and laughing. I wasn't drinking, and found it hard to fit into the conversation.

She did act like "one of the guys" but I believe her drinking has been blown out of proportion. She was drinking and having a good time that night at the Baltimore Civic Arena, but definitely did not become intoxicated. George Hamilton IV, in the book *Patsy: The Life and Times of Patsy Cline*, was quoted as saying "We played a lot of beer joints and honky-tonks and dance halls and I never saw her inebriated. She was always professional. Patsy could take a drink with the rest of us; she could hold her liquor, as they say. But I never can remember ever seeing her mess up a show or miss one. I never even saw her drunk."

I've had to rely on books to learn more about her life and her career. About two years ago, a yearning came over me to know as much about her as possible. She definitely was not the loose woman the way some like to portray her. Yes, she cussed, she was frank in her speech, she was bold (a "no-no" for a woman in the 50s), and I'm sure she made her share of mistakes as most young people do. But I personally witnessed her compassion, her sense of loyalty, how well she treated her friends and fans, and that told me a lot about her character. Early in her career, in a letter to Treva Miller Steinbicker, her first fan club president, she wrote that her all time favorite song was either *Satisfied Mind* or *Just A Closer Walk With Thee*. Although I wasn't around her during her last few years, I'm certain she was someone who would have been learning, growing, and maturing, especially after her spiritual awakening following the 1961 car accident that almost took her life. After that experience, she told gospel singer Wally Fowler that she "got it together with the Lord."

The most heartbreaking thing I learned about Patsy was from the book, *Patsy: The Life and Times of Patsy Cline*. Hilda told Bernard Schwartz, producer of the movie *Sweet Dreams*, what Sam Hensley had done to Patsy: "Schwartz related how Hilda, shaken, but "stoic," opened up the painful subject of Patsy's incestuous relationship with her father, in the conviction that such information was important in understanding her famous, yet often misunderstood daughter, and thus integral to the development of the biopic." It hurt and angered me that Patsy had been a victim of sexual abuse, and that's exactly what it was. And I resented it being referred to as an "incestuous relationship." It was child molestation, not a relationship. I can't repeat here what I said about Sam Hensley.

I hate to think about how awful life must have been with him. Marie's daughter Debbie told me about his horrible behavior when he came with Hilda to her mother's home for dinner. He didn't just cuss, he made blasphemous speeches. He threw a fit when they were ready to leave because he couldn't find his hat. On the next visit, he crudely brought along a tree stump to hang his hat on.

Around 1948, he deserted Hilda and her children—Patsy, Sam "John", and Sylvia. A cousin, Herman Longley, in *Honky Tonk Angel: The Intimate Story of Patsy Cline*, was quoted as saying this about his conversation with Sam concerning the marriage breakup: "He said that there wasn't another woman and hinted that Hilda was seeing another man, but I didn't put much faith in that." He had done something despicable, but yet he accused Hilda. *Patsy: The Life and Times of Patsy Cline* gives this account:

"Their neighbors recalled seeing very little of Sam, as though he were coming and going. Then he left, for good. There was rancor on both sides. In later accounts, Sam bitterly laid the blame for the breakup of the family squarely on Hilda. As far as Hilda was concerned, his insults had been unspeakable. His name was rarely mentioned in Ginny's home again. Indeed, in none of Patsy's own accounts of her early childhood did she ever refer to him or his singing again."

Despite the financial hardship that resulted from his abandonment, Patsy must have felt great relief that he was finally out of their lives. She didn't have any contact with him after that until shortly before his death in 1956. I felt some guilty pangs after I learned how Hensley treated her. As difficult as it had been with my Dad, my childhood had been more secure and pleasant than Patsy's. A remark I once made about Dad when I was mad at him, "Patsy can have him," came back to haunt me. I'm so grateful now that she only experienced the best side of our father. She had already experienced the worst side of a father with Hensley.

If Patsy and Dad had been able to be together more, they probably would have locked horns; they were very much alike. But as it was, they were able to see each other only through rose-colored glasses. "Pop" Brannon most likely came across as the ideal father, and in turn, he no doubt viewed his other daughter the same way. Margaret Jones, in her book about Patsy, explained why Patsy was drawn to boyfriend Jumbo Rinker. Among other things, she stated he had a pilot's license and "liked to drink, have a good time, drive fast, and had a predilection for getting into dazzling wrecks". I found her description of Jumbo eerie. She could have just as well been describing our Dad.

SUPPLEMENT TO THE *EVENING STAR,* 1956

The stars of *Town and Country Jamboree.* Sitting, left to right: Jimmy Dean, Patsy Cline. Standing, left to right: Mary Klick, Dale Turner. *Photo/Collection of Mary Klick Robinson. Copyright Washington Post; reprinted by permission of the DC Public Library*

FORMER CHET BRANNON HOME

Chet built this home on Pennsylvania Ave., Hancock, MD around 1959, after the state took his businesses and home to make way for I-70. This is how the home looks today. The window to the far left was the location of Bob's bedroom where Patsy liked to rest on Bob's bed.
Photo by Charlotte Brannon Bartles

CHET BRANNON'S LAST BUSINESS

This garage and radiator shop was built on Pennsylvania Ave, Hancock, MD after the state took his other business complex to make way for I-70. It was within walking distance of his newly built ranch style brick home. *Photo/Charlotte Brannon Bartles*

CHET AND GLADYS WITH FAMILY

Left to right: Jim Brannon (Chet's brother) and wife Jessie, Gladys Brannon, Chet Brannon, William "Bubber" Hess and wife Maud (Chet's sister), and Lizzie and Tom Brannon (Chet's brother). *Photo/Collection of Charlotte Brannon Bartles*

1960 PHOTO OF CHET BRANNON

It was around this time he bought a farm. He and his family never lived there, but he rented out the farmhouse, planted a garden and raised animals for butchering. After two years, he sold this new venture. *Photo/Collection of Charlotte Brannon Bartles*

5

Heartaches and Losses

Patsy's dream came true. Her hit records *I Fall To Pieces* and *Crazy* established her as a singing star. But on March 5, 1963, the unthinkable happened. The world lost Patsy. She was returning from a benefit concert in Kansas City when the small plane she was traveling in crashed near Camden, TN. Randy Hughes, her manager, was piloting the plane. Hawkshaw Hawkins and Cowboy Copas were the other passengers. They all perished.

I learned what happened from Mom and Dad. I don't know whether someone notified Dad or if he heard it on the radio. I recently learned from Mrs. Truax, widow of Dad's barber Oscar Truax, that Dad met Oscar at the shop that day and said, "I have bad news this morning. My daughter was killed outside of Nashville." He then asked Oscar if he could take him ahead of his other customers as he was getting ready to leave for Nashville. I was accustomed to his unexplained absences and it was typical of him not to inform us of his plans. Hilda, accompanied by a group of family and friends, traveled by car to Nashville. It's possible he went with them.

Patsy's remains were returned to Winchester and the funeral took place there March 10. Dave said Aunt Maud cried her eyes out, but she wasn't planning to attend the funeral because she'd recently had surgery (She ended up in Winchester anyway). Hilda sent a driver to Hancock for her, as she wanted her to baby-sit the little ones during the funeral services. Even though Aunt Maud had been busy raising thirteen children and Hilda had been wrapped up in Patsy's career, they had somehow managed to maintain their close friendship through the years.

Dad did tell me that he and Jim McCormick tried to attend the funeral, but there were thousands of people making the area so congested he never did make it into the funeral home. He watched the procession from the street. After the interment at Shenandoah Memorial Park and the crowds had cleared, he went to her grave and stayed there for quite some time. He and I never had deep conversations, but I could see and feel his grief. I didn't even attempt to go to the funeral.

Some of my co-workers at the London Fog sewing factory in Hancock bad-mouthed me for that. But funerals are for friends and family to honor their deceased loved one and share their grief. I knew I wouldn't be able to do that because of the hordes of people, curiosity seekers, and reporters who would be there, and it was worse than I imagined. In the book, *Honky Tonk Angel: The Intimate Story of Patsy Cline*, it said, "the mob was unruly," "old friends couldn't get into the funeral home," and "members of the family were disgusted with the conduct of a majority of the crowd." I had the months and years ahead to visit Patsy's grave and remember her.

Sammy Moss, one of the pallbearers, wrote and copyrighted *The Patsy Cline Memorial*. It covered her rise to fame from her beginnings in Winchester, her Nashville successes, her tragic death, and featured her music. He broadcasted it on the first anniversary of her death, March 5, 1964 and every year on March 5 for nineteen years. It was played over WCST in Berkeley Springs, WV, a town near Hancock, MD, and other surrounding radio stations. On March 5, 1982, a drunken driver killed his son. He burned the memorial tapes. It was unbearable for him to be reminded of his son's death and Patsy's death on the same date. Mr. Moss died in 1995.

After Patsy's death, Dad was more subdued and evasive with his answer when someone asked him about being Patsy's father but he never denied it. Beverly McCormick Zimmerman recalls the time, around 1966, she was riding in the car with him on the way to a horse race and asked him bluntly if Patsy was his daughter. He did not respond with a "yes" or "no," but after hesitating a few moments he answered, "I fooled around with her mother a lot, but didn't want to hurt Mom." "Mom" was how he referred to my mother. Since he was older and a little wiser, maybe he decided to be a little more discreet out of consideration for the women he loved. I suspect that someone told him to "tone it down."

The decade following Patsy's death was busy with raising my son Jay, who was born in 1962. I also continued to work outside the home. As Mom's health deteriorated due to the bronchiecstasis, I became more involved with her care, and even learned from hospital staff how to give her breathing treatments. Dad did everything he could to help her. He set up oxygen in the bedroom, bathroom, living room, and in the car. Most importantly, he gave her his time and companionship. She would frequently be in and out of intensive care. Her terrible suffering finally ended when she passed away in 1975. She was only fifty-nine years old.

My father missed her enormously. For the first time in his life, he was alone. I've wondered if he ever went to Hilda after Mom's death hoping to reunite with her. If he did, it understandably turned out to be a futile attempt. Many years had passed and many life-altering events had occurred since they were teenagers living in Winchester. It may not have been in a romantic way, but I truly believe they loved each other until the day they died.

I never wanted my parents to remain alone if one of them died, but I never foresaw Dad seeking companionship and comfort by surrounding himself with several young girls. But that's exactly what he did. Young girls, in their late teens, started to hang out at the house, partying and drinking. Not long ago, I came across a picture of one of them sitting on his lap feeding him something. Two of the girls had been Marie's foster children. One day Bob and I went to Dad's to do some chores. I was to do the housecleaning and Bob was to mow the lawn, but neither of us could do our jobs because the fair maidens had total "run of the house." Their presence at Dad's home was the talk of the town. I was the talk of the town after I chased them out of the house that day. Dad wasn't there while that ruckus was going on. There weren't any repercussions, so maybe he was ready for them to be gone. Thankfully, he settled down after that. The lady who had cleaned house for my mother moved in with him and stayed with him until the end.

Shortly after Aunt Maud's husband died in 1981, Dad and Aunt Maud mended their relationship. He hadn't spoken to her for at least fifteen years. Dave told me Dad was mad about something he believed Aunt Maud had said. Aunt Maud denied being the guilty party. She said she knew who made the remark but wasn't telling. Their differences never kept me away from her. Dad took the first step toward reconciliation by sending me on his behalf to find out if she needed anything. After I explained the purpose of my visit, Aunt Maud's eyes filled with tears and she said, "I always loved your Dad." It was then they began to call on one another regularly.

Dad was a good grandfather. He enjoyed spending time with Jay and even took him along a few times when he and Mom vacationed in Florida. Jay had Dad's natural mechanical abilities and love of fast cars. He was a very caring young man, too. One year around Thanksgiving, I came from work to find him bagging food from our cupboards and refrigerator. I asked him what on earth he was doing. He told me about a family that didn't have any food for a Thanksgiving meal, so he was giving them our food, and suggested I bake them a cake. He was the light of our life, and I thought I'd never see light again after a car accident claimed his life in 1983. I had already lost my only other child, Richard Coe, who was born prematurely in 1958 and lived just two days. Jay's death brought sorrow I didn't think I'd be able to endure, but the Lord gave me the strength to get through that devastating time. And Aunt Maud was a great comfort to us. Jay had loved her. He often stayed with her when he was a little boy, and it would be all I could do to get him to come home. My husband Dick and I stayed with her for several weeks after his death.

Tragedy struck my brother Bob's family as well. His sixteen-year-old daughter Kristie died as a result of an inoperable brain tumor on January 9, 1991, the same month and day that Jay died. She was the most courageous young lady I've ever known. We all wanted to be a comfort to her, but she was the one who comforted us.

Perhaps it was due to muscle I'd gained from my own personal ordeal that I was finally able to stand up to Dad. At 6:00 a.m. one morning, he called me at my job, furious with me because of something I'd said to his companion. He told me to apologize or else he would cut me out of his will. Something in me snapped. I told him, "All I ever wanted was you and never got it, so don't hang a dollar over my head." I made the apology, but a wall went up between us that never came down. I had to pay a price for talking back to him. He didn't have anything nice to say about me after that incident and told all his friends from Hancock and Winchester that he was cutting me out of his will. He never did; however, I don't know whether it was because that was never his real intention or because he just hadn't gotten around to doing it.

But he was my father, and I continued to be there for him anytime he needed me. Not long after Jay's death, he began to have heart problems. One day while I was at work, I saw him drive by in his truck with a flat tire. I knew something was wrong. I left work, followed him in my car, and was finally able to get him stopped. He was disoriented and lost in the town where he had lived for the past fifty years. After he was diagnosed with lung cancer, his decline was rapid. Hospice care was given in his home. We set up a hospital bed in the living room so he could have people around him. As he neared death, he did something that I'll never be able to put out of my mind. He put his arm around my waist, slowly raised his hand to the back of my neck, pulled my face down next to his, and repeatedly said, "Please, please." He was confused, and I couldn't understand what he was asking. Was he asking me to forgive him? Or was he asking me to help him? I wasn't able to answer him; I took quite a guilt trip over that. On June 21, 1984, I left from his house to go directly to Aunt Maud's. Just as I arrived there, I heard the firehouse siren summoning an ambulance. I realized what that meant. At the age of seventy-one, Dad was gone.

PLAQUE AT ENTRANCE OF SHENANDOAH MEMORIAL PARK

Shenandoah Memorial Park, Winchester, VA is the location of Patsy's grave and the Memorial Belltower erected in her honor. *Photo by Charlotte Brannon Bartles*

JAY BARTLES
1962-1983

Jay was the son of Charlotte and Dick Bartles and the grandson of Chet and Gladys Brannon.
Photo/Collection of Charlotte Brannon Bartles

CHESTER "CHET" BRANNON AT THE BEACH

He enjoyed warm weather and the ocean. In his later years, he regularly vacationed in Florida. *Photo/Collection of Charlotte Brannon Bartles*

CHARLOTTE ON VACATION

Charlotte drove to Fayetteville, NC in 1967 to visit with her brother Bob, his wife Bonnie, and their son Brad. *Photo/Collection of Charlotte Brannon Bartles*

AUNT MAUD

She was a source of comfort and strength to the Brannon family and a loyal friend to Hilda Hensley. *Photo/Collection of Charlotte Brannon Bartles*

6

Sweet Dreams, Bittersweet Memories

I was taken back in 1981 when I went to see the movie, *Coal Miner's Daughter.* I had no idea Patsy was portrayed in this movie until I saw it on the screen. It was exciting, but the scene in which Loretta Lynn hears on the radio news of Patsy's death stirred my own heartbreaking memories. That movie was largely responsible for renewed interest in Patsy Cline and her music. People who had never heard of Patsy Cline before were motivated to explore her music and to learn all they could about her. She gained legions of new fans, many of which weren't born until after her death. This interest led to the making of the movie *Sweet Dreams,* which was released in 1985. The Winchester, VA scenes were filmed in Martinsburg, WV, approximately twenty-two miles from Winchester, because Martinsburg looked more like Winchester looked during the 1950s. All our area newspapers covered the filming extensively, along with articles about Patsy and interviews with people who had known her. Sadly, Dad was no longer around. He would have been bursting with pride, and perhaps he may have even participated in the interviews.

All the attention about the movie rekindled my desire to know more of what had actually happened between Hilda and my Dad. I got up the nerve to call Hilda, hoping she would volunteer the information now that Hollywood had told Patsy's story. We talked for an hour and a half, starting with a chat about the movie. She said the scene that had Charlie out all night partying while Patsy gave birth to Julie was untrue. She talked about her frustration with what had already been written about Patsy and said, "Why the hell can't they just print the truth?" After that, the conversation shifted to my son Jay and Dad. Hilda and I both had experienced the loss of a dearly loved child. We talked of how our deep grief had affected us. We also reminisced about Chester Brannon. Several times she stated, "Your father was very good to me." I took that to mean that some kind of relationship had existed between them over the years and he had helped her financially as well. But, she never did bring up the subject of their youthful days in Winchester and the birth of Patsy. I didn't take the advice given by the two ladies who came to Dad's sale and told me what Hilda had told them. I couldn't muster the courage to tell Hilda about that incident or even steer the discussion in that direction.

I wanted to see *Sweet Dreams*, but I was hesitant to go for fear that someone from the area would recognize me and start asking questions about Dad and Patsy. Watching that movie would be emotional enough without other memories being dredged up. My girlfriend convinced me to go along with her to see it at a theatre in Hagerstown, MD. It really didn't seem like Patsy to me, it was just someone playing a part. I found it to be both poignant and disturbing, and I can't imagine what it did to Hilda when she saw that movie. I also experienced sadness that my family's relationship to Patsy had never been acknowledged and, most likely, never would be.

Hilda was very tactful but her opinion of *Sweet Dreams* came through loud and clear in an interview for an April 1986 *Winchester Star* newspaper article. When asked how she liked the movie, she answered, "I really don't know how to tell you anything about that. In all justice to the actors, I can't do that. I think Jessica did a wonderful job with what she had to work with. We were told they were going to make a beautiful love story…. I saw it one time. That was enough." She wasn't as reserved when she sat next to Dave at the Brannon family reunion held at the Cacapon State Park, not far from Berkeley Springs, WV. Dave said that when he asked her about *Sweet Dreams*, she stomped her cane down and said, "They made her out to be a cigarette smoking, bar hopping, beer drinking slut." Dave was amused by her choice of words and recalls that at that moment she reminded him of Granny Clampett from the *Beverly Hillbillies*.

Marie invited me to accompany her once when she went to see Hilda. Her house door was unlocked, so we stepped into the living room. She wasn't home and we later learned she had been at a neighbor's house. The first thing I noticed was a huge portrait of Patsy hanging on the wall. That tugged at my heart. The room was very neat, warm, and comfortable.

On another day, I was driving down Kent Street and noticed Hilda sitting in a chair on her porch. I parked my car along the street, got out, and joined her on the porch. She was friendly but did not invite me into the house. We made idle chitchat, and she once again made the statement that my father had been very good to her. She pointed out the two other houses she had lived in, a white one across the street and a red brick one down the street where Patsy had married

Charlie. Again, I didn't ask about her early relationship with Dad. I didn't know how she'd react. But I did have the feeling she knew exactly what was on my mind. She appeared anxious for me to leave. About fifteen minutes after our visit began, I took my cue and left. I had so many questions, and not just about what happened between her and my Dad. For instance, how and when did Patsy learn who her real father was? And, did they stay in touch after she moved to Nashville? Did Patsy ever mention Bob and me? I now understand why Hilda could not have had such a conversation with me. One question would have led to another and possibly taken us into areas neither one of us were prepared to go at that time. So, my questions remain unanswered, and maybe it's just as well.

Aunt Maud and Marie died in 1997. Hilda Hensley died in 1998. The full story will never be known. The details are no longer important to me. I've known since I was a little girl what was most important for me to know. Patsy Cline was my father's daughter and a half-sister to Bob and me. We didn't have the opportunity to grow up together. We led very different lives. Despite that, Patsy was always a presence in my life. I felt Dad wanted me to be like Patsy, not necessarily a singer, but someone who was magnetic, daring, and determined to be successful. I regret that we weren't able to be together more and relate to each other as sisters. I genuinely believe if she hadn't died so young, we would have found a way to build our relationship.

It still stings when I read or watch something about Patsy and there's no mention of the Brannon family. It's been an uphill struggle telling my story because of the doubt and, at times, outright disbelief of others. When I told Charlie Dick my story, he told me that Patsy never told him any of this. Although it's hard to imagine she didn't tell her husband, one has to take into consideration her very close, loyal relationship with Hilda. Charlie also asked if I had proof. No, I don't have DNA tests or any other scientific evidence, but I have the proof I need—what I saw, what I experienced, and what I was told by my parents and other close relatives. What Marie and Aunt Maud refused to discuss spoke volumes. Patsy told her close friend Dottie West about me, and admitted to my good friend, Pearl Younker, that Chester Brannon was her father. Charlie said he has no memory of ever being in my parents' home. My brother Bob, who was there when Charlie visited, was very surprised at that statement and remarked, "He said that? You're kidding." That was over forty years ago, and I guess Charlie was more memorable to us than we were to him. I've mailed certified letters to a couple of important people in Patsy's life; I've yet to receive any replies. I spoke by phone with one gentleman who's been very involved with Patsy related projects in Winchester. He was quite harsh and gave me these instructions,

"Write what you want to about her, but keep it in your own family. Don't go public with it."

Fortunately, there are others who have been encouraging and supportive. Mary Klick Robinson, who had been a Town and Country Jamboree co-star, was very kind and helpful even though she said Patsy never told her about my father. It meant a great deal to me that she did not dismiss me or question the truthfulness of my story. Courage to proceed with this project came after I spoke with someone from the Always, Patsy Cline Fan Club in Winchester. He spoke the words that reinforced my conviction I was doing the right thing: "Patsy is a true legend. You have the true story on her and a book with the truth should go with her through the coming years."

The true story will alter Patsy's official biography and will be difficult for some to accept. But I think the truth should prevail over someone's comfort level and the need to keep her life story "as is." It should be a consolation to Patsy's fans to know that Patsy knew a father who loved and adored her, regardless of how limited his role had been.

Perhaps Hilda had planned to tell this story in her own time and in her own way. She did write her memoirs in her later years, but they've yet to be published. In 1997, during Marie's viewing at the Giffin Funeral Home, she found her own way to give me confirmation of what she knew I'd known all along. Mourners had to walk up a step to enter the viewing room. Hilda was getting ready to step down as I approached to enter. She stopped, leaned down close to my face, touched her nose to mine, and, as her eyes teared, she looked intensely into my eyes. Her message was clear when she then spoke the words, "Your eyes, your brown eyes." With that said, she walked away.

December 11, 1998

Hilda Hensley Dies; Family, Friends Praise Patsy Cline's Mother

By DON WORTHINGTON and WAYDE BYARD
The Winchester Star

One of the last — and perhaps greatest — living links to Winchester's most famous citizen is dead.

Hilda Hensley, the mother of country music legend Patsy Cline, died at age 82 Thursday in Winchester Medical Center.

Funeral arrangements for Mrs. Hensley with Jones Funeral Home are incomplete.

"She worshipped me as a mother, and I worshipped her as a daughter," Mrs. Hensley said in a 1986 interview in The Winchester Star.

And she was loved by her family.

"When I came to visit, I came to visit Granny. I did not come to visit Mrs. Hensley, I did not come to visit Patsy Cline's mother, I visited my Granny," Hensley's granddaughter, Julie Fudge, said this morning from Nashville.

"That's the way I liked it and the way she liked it."

"She was a very simple person, who would always say, "Don't do a lot for me," said Fudge, who lived with Mrs. Hensley for several years after her mother died in a 1963 plane crash.

"She was always so busy, cooking and caring for us, you could not make her slow down," Fudge said.

Mrs. Hensley was 16 when she gave birth to the future singing

Hilda Hensley is shown at a Patsy Cline fan club tribute dinner in Winchester in 1989.

Star Photo by Rick Foster

star on Sept. 8, 1932.

In another Star interview, in 1989, she said they grew up together "more like sisters than like mother and daughter."

"She was full of life, just like Patsy was," Charlie Dick, Cline's second husband, said this morning from Nashville.

George Hamilton IV, one of Cline's co-stars, said this morning from Nashville, "She was a strong Southern woman who, with a lot of love, care and encouragement had a great deal to do with her daughter becoming a star."

Patsy Cline died in a plane crash on March 5, 1963, near Camden, Tenn. At 30, her popularity was just cresting with hits such as "Crazy," "Sweet Dreams," and "Walking After Midnight."

"She never got over Patsy's death," Dick said this morning.

Her popularity surged anew after she was portrayed by Beverly

See Hilda Hensley Page A8

Hilda Hensley

D'Angelo in the 1980 film "Coal Miner's Daughter."

In 1985, Oscar winner Jessica Lange portrayed Cline in the film "Sweet Dreams." Ed Harris played her husband, Charlie Dick, and Anne Wedgeworth played Mrs. Hensley. Martinsburg, W.Va., doubled for Winchester when location filming was done locally.

Mrs. Hensley was shown the film at a private screening.

"I really don't know how to tell you anything about that," she said. "In all justice to the actors, I can't do that. I think Jessica did a wonderful job with what she had to work with."

Lange received an Academy Award nomination for her portrayal of Cline.

Still, it was obvious that Mrs. Hensley was not completely satisfied with the film.

"We were told they were going to make a beautiful love story. . . . I saw it one time. That was enough."

In a similar vein, Mrs. Hensley often displayed ambivalence toward Winchester's efforts to honor her famous daughter. In 1986, in another Star interview, Mrs. Hensley talked of the city's efforts to name a street after her daughter (something that has since come to pass).

"I have kept quiet. I thought my absence in these things would convey my feelings. . . . It's a very nice gesture, but I think it's way too late. . . . If they wanted to do something in her memory — let's

face it, they can't do anything for Patsy now."

Mrs. Hensley favored setting up a scholarship in Cline's memory, dedicated to helping someone like the late singer "who had no help but did have talent."

The Winchester-based Patsy Cline Foundation annually presents scholarships in the singer's memory.

The foundation also annually holds a graveside service during the local Labor Day weekend festivities that honor Cline.

In 1989, Mrs. Hensley talked about why she had decided to participate in the annual three-day celebration of her daughter's life held locally.

"Last year, at the fan club

meeting, I realized how much people really love my daughter. Some had ridden the bus from Canada to be here. I feel like I'd be letting my daughter's fans down if I didn't help."

Even after her daughter's rise to popularity and subsequent rediscovery, Mrs. Hensley lived in a simple two-story house on South Kent Street. She received a small payment from the makers of "Sweet Dreams," but no royalties from the sale of Cline's music. Those went to Dick and Cline's two children.

Mrs. Hensley, however, largely kept to herself in the years after her daughter's death.

"She never got over Patsy's death,' Dick said.

Dick and his brother Mel, of Winchester, remembered her as a caring woman, who had a close relationship with their mother, Mary.

Mary Dick did not drive, and it was Hilda who would pick her up and take her place, Mel Dick said.

"I remember my mother once took a trip to Tennessee and she came back in a snowstorm. Hilda went out to pick her up when no one else was driving," he said.

Ron Morris, managing editor of The Winchester Star, said of Mrs. Hensley, "She was truly a lovely woman. I admired and respected her strong will, her independence, and her unwavering devotion to her daughter."

SECOND PAGE OF DECEMBER 11, 1998 NEWSPAPER ARTICLE

COLLECTION OF CHARLOTTE BRANNON BARTLES/REPRINTED BY PERMISSION OF THE WINCHESTER STAR

ROBERT "BOB" BRANNON AND HIS LOVELY WIFE BONNIE IN 2005

Photo by Mrs. Paul Hull/Collection of Mr. And Mrs. Robert Brannon

CHARLOTTE BRANNON BARTLES IN 2005

PATSY'S ACHIEVEMENTS AND LEGACY♫

Patsy Cline recordings have gone platinum many times over, and forty-two years after her death, continue to sell. She received awards and recognition in her lifetime and posthumously. To learn more about Patsy and her remarkable career, refer to the resources listed in the bibliography. On the Internet, a couple of outstanding sites are www.patsy.nu and www.patsified.com. The following are only a few of her many awards and honors:

1957	*Walkin' After Midnight*, first hit record, which reached #2 on the country charts and #12 on the pop charts. Patsy was the forerunner of "crossover" artists.
1961 and 1962	#1 Female Artist
1962	#1 Hit, *I Fall To Pieces*
1973	Induction into the Country Music Hall of Fame, the first solo female artist to receive such an honor
1992	Induction into the Grammy Hall of Fame for *Crazy*
1993	U.S. Postal Service issued a Commemorative Patsy Cline Stamp
1999	Received a Star on the Hollywood Walk of Fame
2002	#1 on Country Music Television's Countdown of the 40 Greatest Women in Country Music
2004	Country Music Television's Countdown of the Greatest Love Songs in Country Music

#3 Sweet Dreams
#18 I Fall To Pieces

I know it would please Patsy and make her very proud that Hilda Hensley's name is known and revered by her fans just as Gladys Presley's name is known and revered by Elvis fans. Hilda was a very private person, but she did open her heart, and occasionally, her home to fans. She recognized their genuine love and respect for Patsy and knew they would be the ones who would ultimately keep her beloved daughter's flame blazing. Every Labor Day weekend since 1988, fan club members have gathered in Winchester for banquets, memorial services, meetings, and other special events to celebrate Patsy. Fans make the pilgrimage at other times of the year as well, sometimes by the busload. Some make the trip for very personal reasons. The Winchester Star newspaper, in its May 28, 2005 edition, did a story about a couple from Missouri who, accompanied by two carloads of family members, drove more than fourteen hours to be wed in the Kent Street house where Patsy and Charlie were married in 1957. Several other couples had previously married on the porch of the home, but this was the first wedding to take place inside. The current owner invited them in when a steady rain began to fall. Judy Sue Huyett-Kempf, a board member of Celebrating Patsy Cline, Inc., performed the ceremony.

Celebrating Patsy Cline, Inc. is a non-profit corporation committed to perpetuating the memory of Patsy Cline through the establishment of a Patsy Cline Museum in Winchester, VA. In 2003, the group paid $25,000 for three pieces of Patsy's clothing from Hilda's estate, which were on the auction block at Christie's in New York. Hilda's children, Sylvia Wilt and Samuel Hensley, had been battling over their mother's estate in court since 2001. A Winchester circuit court judge ordered the sale of Patsy's clothing to cover the cost of administering the estate. The sixteen clothing items that were auctioned in 2003 netted $123,919. Hopefully, many of those items purchased will be donated to the Patsy Cline Museum, which is scheduled to open in March 2006 at 48 S. Loudoun St., Winchester, VA. It was Hilda's dream to have a museum to honor her beloved daughter's life and career.

On September 3, 2005, an historical highway marker was unveiled during a ceremony at Patsy's childhood home on 608 South Kent Street. Celebrating Patsy Cline, Inc. paid for the marker and organized the event. The next goal is to get the modest home onto the National Register of Historic Places. Mayor Elizabeth A. Minor stated, "This represents a significant milestone for the city of Winchester. It's long overdue." Patsy's family and fans couldn't agree more.

Celebrating Patsy Cline, Inc.

P.O. Box 3900

Winchester, Virginia 22604

www.celebratingpatsycline.org

Always Patsy Cline Fan Club
P. O. Box 2236
Winchester, Virginia 22604

BIBLIOGRAPHY

BOOKS

Bego, Mark. *I Fall To Pieces: The Music and Life of Patsy Cline.* Holbrook, MA: Adams Media Corp., 1996

Brown, Stuart E., and Lorraine F. Myers. *Singing Girl from the Shenandoah Valley.* Berryville, VA: Virginia Book Company, 1996.

Hazen, Cindy, and Mike Freeman. *Love Always, Patsy.* New York, New York: The Berkley Publishing Group, 1999.

Jones, Margaret. *Patsy: The Life and Times of Patsy Cline.* New York, New York: HarperPerennial, 1995.

Nassour, Ellis. *Patsy Cline.* New York, New York: Tower Publications, 1981.

Nassour, Ellis. *Honky Tonk Angel: The Intimate Story of Patsy Cline.* New York, New York: St. Martin's Press, 1993.

NEWSPAPERS

HANCOCK NEWS.	March 9, 1983.	"An Irony to Painful to Bear" by Linda Swaim-Buzzerd.
HERALD MAIL.	October 18, 1992.	"An Overdue Honor?" by Kathy Boccella.
WINCHESTER STAR.		
	April 1986.	"Patsy's Mom," Column One by Ron Morris.
	December 11, 1998.	"Hilda Hensley Dies; Family, Friends Praise Patsy Cline's Mother" By Don Worthington and Wayne Byard.
	March 1, 2002.	"Who Owns Patsy Cline's Clothes?" by Stephanie K. Moran.
	November 23, 2002.	"Patsy Cline Items To Be Auctioned" by Stephanie M. Mangino.
	November 19, 2003.	"Patsy Cline's Clothing Attracts High Bidders" By Stephanie M. Mangino.

July 23, 2004.	"Cline Siblings Choose Items From Estate" by Stephanie M. Mangino.
August 20, 2004.	"Cline Court Battle Wrapping Up" by Stephanie M. Mangino.
August 31, 2004.	"Always Patsy Cline Weekend in Winchester" by Melanie Mullinax
May 28, 2005.	"A 'Sweet Dream' Comes True for Patsy Cline Fan" by Stephanie M. Mangino.
July 14, 2005.	"On the Trail of Patsy Cline" by F. C. Lowe.
September 6, 2005.	"Marker Unveiling Tops Annual Trek for Cline" by Charlie Jackson.

978-0-595-37324
0-595-37324-0

Made in the USA
Las Vegas, NV
05 November 2023

80295935R00059